W9-BMT-085

30 minute
italian

p

This is a Parragon Publishing Book
First published in 2005

Parragon Publishing
Queen Street House
4 Queen Street
Bath, BA1 1HE, UK

Copyright © Parragon 2005

All rights reserved. No part of this publication may be reproduced, stored
in a retrieval system, or transmitted, in any form or by any means, electronic,
mechanical, photocopying, recording, or otherwise, without the prior
permission of the copyright holder.

ISBN: 1-40545-318-4

Printed in China

Produced by the Bridgewater Book Company Ltd

Notes for the Reader
This book uses imperial, metric, and US cup measurements. Follow the same
units of measurement throughout; do not mix imperial and metric. All spoon
measurements are level: teaspoons are assumed to be 5 ml, and tablespoons
are assumed to be 15 ml. Unless otherwise stated, milk is assumed to be whole,
eggs and individual fruits such as bananas are medium, and pepper is freshly
ground black pepper.

Recipes using raw or very lightly cooked eggs should be avoided by infants,
the elderly, pregnant women, convalescents, and anyone suffering from an
illness. Pregnant and breast-feeding women are advised to avoid eating
peanuts and peanut products.

Contents

Introduction

Bring an authentic taste of Italy into your life, wherever you live, in 30 minutes or less with this special collection of recipes. Scoring high on style yet low on time and effort, there are classic and contemporary-style appetizers, entrées, light meals, and desserts for everyday eating, alfresco dining, and easy entertaining. These aren't quick-fixes or shortcuts—just great Italian food.

QUALITY & SIMPLICITY These are the essentials of Italian cooking, using high-quality ingredients and simple techniques, which is how you can produce such delicious meals in minutes. But first you need those vital ingredients.

FRESH FLAVORS There is nothing to match herbs for effortlessly fast-forwarding the flavor of food, particularly if you use fresh rather than dried herbs. Basil is the most important herb in Italian cooking, but flat-leaf parsley, oregano, and rosemary play key roles. Fresh garlic is also a must—avoid any bulbs with green shoots, and discard any green centers to the cloves, which bitter the flavor. Fresh tomatoes are another central ingredient, and whether plum, cherry, or beefsteak, look for ripeness and sun-ripened or on-the-vine varieties. Luscious fresh figs perfectly partner prosciutto, while juicy, fragrant peaches are complemented by silken mascarpone cheese.

CHILLER TREATS Paper-thin slices of prosciutto crudo, or "raw ham" (but salt-cured and air-dried), reign supreme over the antipasto platter, but its sweet flesh also adds a distinctive flavor to a creamy pasta sauce—it requires minimal cooking,

otherwise it will toughen. It also makes an ideal salad ingredient. Cheese is the other Italian chiller staple. A block of tightly foil-wrapped, grainy Parmesan, ready to be freshly grated or peeled into shavings, will keep for several weeks in the refrigerator. Mozzarella has a much shorter shelf-life, but its creamy texture and melting qualities have culinary applications way beyond pizza here, from salads to bruschetta and fondue.

PANTRY PLEASURES Many of the quality ingredients used in these recipes are in fact pantry items, so start stocking up now, beginning with olive oil for cooking and the finest, fruity extra virgin olive oil for dressings, along with bottled olives and capers. Good-quality dried pasta—make sure it says "durum wheat" on the label—is often superior to fresh, which can vary greatly in quality. And there is no substitute for real risotto rice for achieving that desirable creamy consistency. Canned anchovies add a depth of flavor to many dishes, while bottled artichoke hearts and roasted bell peppers make excellent instant ingredients for pasta dishes and salads. Sun-dried tomatoes packed in oil provide an intense hit of sweet fruitiness straight from southern Italy.

Soups & Appetizers

This satisfying soup makes a good lunch or supper dish and you can use any

vegetables that you have at hand. Children will love the tiny pasta shapes.

Chicken & Vegetable Soup

serves 6

12 oz/350 g skinless, boneless chicken breasts

2 tbsp sunflower oil

1 onion, diced

1½ cups carrots, diced

9 oz/250 g cauliflower florets

3¾ cups chicken stock

2 tsp dried mixed herbs

4½ oz/125 g small dried pasta shapes, such as conchigliette or ditalini

salt and pepper

TO SERVE

freshly grated Parmesan cheese (optional)

crusty bread

Using a sharp knife, finely dice the chicken.

Heat the oil in a large pan over medium–high heat, add the chicken and vegetables, and cook, stirring frequently, for 5 minutes, or until the onion is soft and the chicken is lightly browned.

Stir in the stock and herbs. Bring to a boil and add the pasta. Return to a boil, then reduce the heat, cover, and let simmer for 10 minutes, stirring occasionally to prevent the pasta sticking together.

Season to taste with salt and pepper and sprinkle with Parmesan cheese, if using. Serve with crusty bread.

soups & appetizers

The Calabrian mountains in southern Italy

provide large amounts of wild mushrooms that

are rich in flavor and color.

Calabrian Mushroom Soup

serves 4

2 tbsp olive oil

1 onion, chopped

1 lb/450 g mixed mushrooms, such as cèpe, oyster, and white

1¼ cups milk

3¾ cups hot vegetable stock

8 slices Italian or rustic bread

2 garlic cloves, crushed

3 tbsp butter, melted

2¾ oz/75 g finely grated Gruyère cheese

salt and pepper

Heat the oil in a large skillet over medium–high heat, add the onion and cook, stirring frequently, for 3–4 minutes until soft and golden.

Wipe each mushroom with a damp cloth and cut any large mushrooms into smaller, bite-size pieces.

Add the mushrooms to the pan, stirring quickly to coat them in the oil.

Add the milk to the pan and bring to a boil. Reduce the heat, cover, and let simmer for 5 minutes. Gradually stir in the hot stock and season to taste with salt and pepper.

Meanwhile, toast the bread lightly on both sides under a broiler preheated to medium.

Mix the garlic and butter together in a bowl and spoon generously over the toast.

Place the toast in the bottom of a large tureen or divide it between 4 individual serving bowls and pour the hot soup over. Top with the Gruyère cheese and serve immediately.

A *minestra* is a soup, normally one of medium thickness. In this hearty lentil soup

farfalline, a small bow-shaped variety of pasta, makes it a meal in itself.

Minestra di Lentiche

serves 4

4 lean bacon strips, cut into small squares

1 onion, chopped

2 garlic cloves, crushed

2 celery stalks, chopped

¼ cup dried farfalline or spaghetti broken into small pieces

14½ oz/410 g canned brown lentils, drained

5 cups hot ham or vegetable stock

2 tbsp chopped fresh mint

Place the bacon, onion, garlic, and celery in a preheated large skillet over medium–high heat. Dry-fry for 4–5 minutes, stirring frequently, until the onion is soft and the bacon is just beginning to brown.

Add the pasta to the pan and cook, stirring, for 1 minute to coat well in the oil.

Add the lentils and stock and bring to a boil. Reduce the heat and let simmer for 12–15 minutes until the pasta is tender.

Remove from the heat and stir in the mint.

Transfer the soup to warmed soup bowls and serve immediately.

These tasty little tomato and mozzarella cheese toasts can be served as finger food at a party or as an appetizer. Remember to switch on the oven and broiler to preheat before you start the preparation.

Bruschetta

serves 4

2 small ciabatta loaves

¾ cup sun-dried tomato paste

10 oz/280 g mozzarella cheese, diced

1 tbsp chopped fresh oregano

2 tbsp olive oil

pepper

mixed salad greens, to serve

Preheat the oven to 425°F/220°C and preheat the broiler to medium. Slice the bread diagonally, discarding the end crusts, to give a total of about 24 slices. Toast the bread lightly on both sides under the preheated broiler.

Spread the tomato paste evenly onto 1 side of each slice of toast, then top each with the mozzarella cheese.

Place the bruschetta on a large cookie sheet and sprinkle with the oregano. Season to taste with pepper and drizzle with the oil. Bake in the preheated oven for 5 minutes, or until the mozzarella has melted. Let stand for 2 minutes, then serve warm with mixed salad greens.

Deep-fried seafood is a popular dish all round

the Mediterranean, where fish of every shape

and flavor are fresh and abundant.

Deep-Fried Seafood

serves 4

7 oz/200 g prepared squid

7 oz/200 g jumbo shrimp, shelled and deveined

5½ oz/150 g smelt

oil, for deep-frying

generous ¼ cup all-purpose flour

1 tsp dried basil

salt and pepper

TO SERVE

garlic mayonnaise

lemon wedges

Rinse the squid, shrimp, and smelt under cold running water to remove any dirt or grit. Using a sharp knife, slice the squid into rings, leaving the tentacles whole.

Heat the oil in a large pan to 350–375°F/180–190°C, or until a cube of bread browns in 30 seconds.

Place the flour in a bowl, add the basil, and season to taste with salt and pepper. Mix well. Roll the squid, shrimp, and smelt in the seasoned flour until coated. Shake off any excess flour.

Cook the seafood in the hot oil, in batches, for 2–3 minutes, or until crispy and golden all over. Remove all of the seafood with a slotted spoon and let drain thoroughly on paper towels.

Transfer the seafood to serving plates and serve with garlic mayonnaise and a few lemon wedges.

soups & appetizers

Crostini means "little toasts" in Italian, though it can also refer to canapés served on toast such as this delicious liver appetizer.

Crostini alla Fiorentina

serves 4

3 tbsp olive oil

1 onion, chopped

1 celery stalk, chopped

1 carrot, chopped

1–2 garlic cloves, crushed

4½ oz/125 g chicken livers

4½ oz/125 g calf's, lamb's, or pig's liver

⅔ cup red wine

1 tbsp tomato paste

2 tbsp chopped fresh parsley, plus extra to garnish

3–4 canned anchovy fillets, drained, rinsed, and finely chopped

2 tbsp stock or water

2–3 tbsp butter

1 tbsp capers, drained and rinsed

salt and pepper

fried crusty bread, to serve

Heat the oil in a pan over low heat, add the onion, celery, carrot, and garlic, and cook, stirring frequently, for 4–5 minutes until the onion is soft but not colored.

Meanwhile, rinse and dry the chicken and calf's livers. Slice the calf's liver into strips. Add the livers to the pan and cook, stirring, for a few minutes until well sealed on all sides.

Add half the wine and cook until it has mostly evaporated. Then add the remaining wine, the tomato paste, half the parsley, anchovies, stock, and salt and pepper to taste.

Cover the pan and simmer, stirring occasionally, for 15–20 minutes until the liver is tender and most of the liquid has been absorbed.

Let the mixture cool a little, then either coarsely chop or place in a blender or food processor and process to a chunky purée.

Return to the pan and add the butter, capers, and remaining parsley. Heat through until the butter melts. Turn out into a bowl. Serve warm or cold, spread on the fried bread pieces and sprinkled with parsley.

In the weekly street markets that characterize Italian life, you are sure to find

flavored olives. Ingredients vary with the regions—here are two ideas.

Flavored Olives

each fills a 2¼-cup preserving jar

fresh herb sprigs,
to garnish

CHILI & LEMON OLIVES

3 dried red chilies

1 tsp black peppercorns

1¾ cups black olives in brine

2 lemon slices

1 tsp black mustard seeds

1 tbsp garlic-flavored olive oil

extra virgin olive oil

CILANTRO & BELL PEPPER OLIVES

½ grilled or roasted red or orange bell pepper

scant 1 cup black olives in brine

scant 1 cup green pimento-stuffed olives in brine

1 tbsp capers in brine, rinsed

pinch of dried chili flakes

4 tbsp coarsely chopped fresh cilantro leaves

1 bay leaf

extra virgin olive oil

To make the Chili & Lemon Olives, place the chilies and peppercorns in a mortar and lightly crush with a pestle. Drain and rinse the olives, then pat dry with paper towels. Place all the ingredients in a 2¼-cup preserving jar and pour over enough extra virgin olive oil to cover.

Seal the jar and leave for at least 10 days before serving, shaking the jar daily.

To make the Cilantro & Bell Pepper Olives, finely chop the bell pepper. Drain and rinse the olives, then pat dry with paper towels.

Place all the ingredients in a 2¼-cup preserving jar and pour over enough oil to cover. Seal and let marinate as above.

To serve, spoon into a bowl and garnish with herb sprigs.

This is a typical antipasto dish, with cold cured meats, stuffed olives, and fresh tomatoes, dressed with fresh basil and balsamic vinegar.

Antipasto Platter

serves 4

4 plum tomatoes

1 tbsp balsamic vinegar

6 canned anchovy fillets, drained and rinsed

2 tbsp capers, drained and rinsed

1 cup pitted green olives

6 oz/175 g mixed cured sliced meats, such as prosciutto, pancetta, and salami

8 fresh basil leaves

1 tbsp extra virgin olive oil

salt and pepper

crusty bread, to serve

Using a sharp knife, cut the tomatoes into even slices. Sprinkle the tomato slices with the balsamic vinegar and salt and pepper to taste and set aside.

Chop the anchovies into pieces measuring about the same length as the olives.

Push a piece of anchovy and a caper into the cavity of each olive.

Arrange the sliced meats on 4 individual serving plates with the tomatoes, stuffed olives, and basil leaves.

Lightly drizzle the oil over the ingredients.

Serve the antipasto with plenty of crusty bread.

This classic Italian appetizer is simplicity itself, but it never fails to please. It would be the perfect choice to start an alfresco meal. Find Parma ham or San Daniele, as these are the finest prosciuttos.

Prosciutto & Figs

serves 4

8 ripe fresh figs

8 thin slices prosciutto, about 6 oz/175 g

pepper

Using a sharp knife, cut each fig downward into quarters from the stalk end, but without cutting all the way through. Gently open out each fruit like a flower and place 2 on each of 4 large serving plates.

Arrange 2 slices of prosciutto in decorative folds beside the figs on each plate.

Season well with pepper and serve at room temperature, offering the pepper shaker at the same time.

These deep-fried mozzarella sandwiches are a tasty snack at any time of the day,

or serve cut into smaller triangles as an antipasto with drinks.

Mozzarella Snacks

serves 4

8 slices bread, preferably slightly stale, crusts removed

3½ oz/100 g mozzarella cheese, thickly sliced

⅓ cup black olives, chopped

8 canned anchovy fillets, drained, rinsed, and chopped

16 fresh basil leaves

4 eggs, beaten

⅔ cup milk

oil, for deep-frying

salt and pepper

Cut each slice of bread into 2 triangles. Top 8 of the bread triangles with the mozzarella cheese, olives, and anchovies.

Place the basil leaves on top and season to taste with salt and pepper.

Lay the other 8 triangles of bread over the top and press down around the edges to seal.

Mix the eggs and milk together in a pitcher and pour into a baking dish. Add the sandwiches and let soak for 5 minutes.

Heat the oil in a large pan to 350–375°F/180–190°C, or until a cube of bread browns in 30 seconds.

Before cooking the sandwiches, squeeze the edges together again.

Carefully add the sandwiches, in small batches, to the oil and deep-fry, turning once, for 2 minutes, or until golden. Remove the sandwiches with a slotted spoon and drain on paper towels. Serve immediately while still hot.

This is the Italian version of an omelet, with the additional ingredients mixed into the beaten eggs and the cooking completed under a broiler.

Spinach, Onion & Herb Frittata

serves 6–8

4 tbsp olive oil

6 scallions, sliced

9 oz/250 g young spinach leaves, any coarse stems removed, rinsed

6 large eggs

3 tbsp finely chopped mixed fresh herbs, such as flat-leaf parsley, thyme, and cilantro

2 tbsp freshly grated Parmesan cheese, plus extra shavings to garnish

salt and pepper

fresh flat-leaf parsley sprigs, to garnish

mixed salad, to serve

Heat the oil in a preheated 10-inch/25-cm skillet, preferably non-stick with a flameproof handle, over medium heat. Add the scallions and cook, stirring, for 2 minutes. Add the spinach with only the water that clings to its leaves and cook until it wilts.

Beat the eggs together in a large bowl and season generously with salt and pepper. Using a slotted spoon, transfer the spinach and scallions to the bowl of eggs and stir in the chopped herbs. Pour the excess oil left in the skillet into a heatproof pitcher, then scrape off the crusty bits from the bottom of the pan.

Heat 2 tablespoons of the reserved oil in the skillet. Pour in the egg mixture, smoothing it into an even layer. Cook for 6 minutes, shaking the pan occasionally, or until the underside is set when you lift up the side with a spatula.

Sprinkle the top of the frittata with the Parmesan cheese. Place the pan under a broiler preheated to medium–high and cook for 3 minutes, or until the egg has set on top and the cheese is golden.

Remove the pan from the broiler and slide the frittata onto a serving plate. Let cool for at least 5 minutes before cutting into wedges and garnishing with Parmesan cheese shavings and parsley sprigs. Serve hot, warm, or at room temperature with a mixed salad.

Pasta & Rice

Italy's signature rice dish comes in many guises,

but the basic ingredients and cooking technique

Basic Risotto

are the same. Using a specialty rice, traditionally

arborio, the result is a creamy consistency but

with the grains retaining some of their firmness.

serves 4

8 cups chicken or vegetable stock

3 tbsp butter

1 tbsp olive oil

1 small onion, finely chopped

2¼ cups risotto rice

1 cup freshly grated Parmesan cheese or Grana Padano

salt and pepper

Place the stock in a large pan and bring to a boil, then reduce the heat and let simmer gently over low heat while you are cooking the risotto. Melt 2 tablespoons of the butter with the oil in a deep pan over medium heat. Add the onion and cook, stirring frequently, until soft and starting to turn golden. Do not brown.

Add the rice and stir to coat in the butter and oil. Cook, stirring constantly, for 2–3 minutes until the grains are translucent. Add a ladleful of the hot stock, stirring constantly and increasing the heat to medium so that the liquid bubbles until it is absorbed. Continue adding the remaining stock a ladleful at a time until all the liquid is absorbed—this should take 20 minutes. Season to taste with salt and pepper, but don't add too much salt as the Parmesan cheese is salty.

Remove the risotto from the heat and add the remaining butter. Mix well, then add the Parmesan cheese and stir until it has melted. Adjust the seasoning, if necessary, and serve immediately.

Fresh basil, with its powerfully perfumed flavor, is central to Italian cooking. Here,

some of the leaves are reserved for adding at the end to maximize its impact.

Basil Risotto

serves 4

1 quantity Basic Risotto

10–12 fresh basil leaves

4 fresh tomatoes, seeded and diced

4 oz/115 g green beans, cooked

2 tbsp pine nuts, to garnish

Prepare the Basic Risotto, shredding half the basil and adding to the pan with the tomatoes and beans along with the onion at the very beginning. Cook the vegetables together gently, stirring, for 2–3 minutes to let the flavors blend before adding the rice.

While the risotto is cooking, heat a dry skillet over high heat. Add the pine nuts and cook, stirring, for 1–2 minutes, or until just starting to brown. Be careful not to let them burn.

When the risotto is cooked, tear and carefully fold in half the remaining basil

Serve the risotto in individual bowls, sprinkled with the toasted pine nuts and the remaining whole basil leaves to garnish.

The vivid green color and fragrant flavor of the fresh herbs make this simple risotto

a perfect summertime dish. Oregano, basil, and flat-leaf parsley is a classic Italian

combination, but you could use thyme or lemon thyme instead of oregano.

Herb Risotto

serves 4

1 quantity Basic Risotto

1 zucchini, peeled and diced

large handful mixed fresh herbs, finely chopped

Prepare the Basic Risotto, adding the zucchini to the pan along with the onion at the very beginning.

Carefully fold most of the herbs into the risotto 5 minutes before the end of cooking time.

Serve the risotto on individual plates, sprinkled with the remaining herbs to garnish.

The red wine gives the rice an attractive pinkish tinge, while the sun-dried tomatoes

contribute a concentrated sweetness and chewy texture. Use the variety that comes

Red Wine, Herb & Sun-Dried Tomato Risotto

packed in oil rather than the dry-packed kind, which needs presoaking before it

can be added to a dish.

serves 4

1 quantity Basic Risotto, made with a mixture of half strong Italian red wine and half vegetable stock

6 sun-dried tomatoes, finely chopped

1 tbsp chopped fresh thyme, plus extra sprigs to garnish

1 tbsp chopped fresh flat-leaf parsley

10–12 basil leaves, shredded, to garnish

Prepare the Basic Risotto, adding the sun-dried tomatoes to the pan along with the onion at the very beginning and using a mixture of half red wine and half vegetable stock.

Carefully fold the herbs into the risotto 5 minutes before the end of cooking time.

Serve the risotto on individual plates, garnished with the shredded basil and thyme sprigs.

Homemade pesto is much more delicious than even good-quality, store-bought

brands and it makes a wonderful nocook sauce for all types of freshly cooked

pasta. Use romano cheese in place of the Parmesan cheese for an extra tang.

Pasta with Pesto

serves 4

1 lb/450 g dried tagliatelle

salt

fresh basil sprigs, to garnish

PESTO

2 garlic cloves

scant ¼ cup pine nuts

large pinch of sea salt

4 oz/115 g fresh basil leaves

½ cup olive oil

½ cup freshly grated Parmesan cheese

To make the pesto, place the garlic, pine nuts, and sea salt in a blender or food processor and process briefly. Add the basil leaves and process to a paste. With the motor running, gradually add the oil. Scrape into a bowl and beat in the Parmesan cheese. Season to taste with salt. Alternatively, put the garlic, pine nuts, sea salt, and basil leaves into a mortar and crush with a pestle to make a paste. Transfer to a bowl, work in the Parmesan cheese, then gradually add the oil, beating with a wooden spoon. Season to taste with salt.

Bring a large pan of lightly salted water to a boil. Add the pasta, return to a boil, and cook for 8–10 minutes, or until tender but still firm to the bite. Drain well, return to the pan, and toss with half the pesto. Divide between warmed serving plates and top with the remaining pesto. Garnish with basil sprigs and serve.

This famous Roman recipe is probably the simplest pasta dish in the world—

spaghetti with olive oil and garlic.

Spaghetti Olio e Aglio

serves 4

1 lb/450 g dried spaghetti

½ cup extra virgin olive oil

3 garlic cloves, finely chopped

3 tbsp chopped fresh flat-leaf parsley

salt and pepper

Bring a large, heavy-bottom pan of lightly salted water to a boil. Add the pasta, return to a boil, and cook for 8–10 minutes, or until tender but still firm to the bite.

Meanwhile, heat the oil in a heavy-bottom skillet over low heat. Add the garlic and a pinch of salt and cook, stirring constantly, for 3–4 minutes until golden. Do not let the garlic brown or it will taste bitter. Remove from the heat.

Drain the pasta and transfer to a large, warmed serving dish. Pour in the garlic-flavored oil, then add the parsley and season to taste with salt and pepper. Toss well and serve immediately.

Quick, easy, utterly delicious, and full of sunshine colors and flavors, this is the perfect

dish for any occasion, whether it is a family supper or an informal dinner party.

Pasta with Sun-Dried Tomatoes

serves 4

12 oz/350 g dried tagliatelle

1 tbsp olive oil

2 pieces of sun-dried tomatoes in oil, drained and thinly sliced

2 tbsp sun-dried tomato paste

1 cup dry white wine

2 oz/55 g radicchio leaves, shredded

salt and pepper

3 scallions, thinly sliced

3 tbsp lightly toasted pine nuts

Bring a large, heavy-bottom pan of lightly salted water to a boil. Add the pasta, return to a boil, and cook for 8–10 minutes, or until tender but still firm to the bite.

Meanwhile, heat half the olive oil in a large, heavy-bottom skillet. Add the tomatoes and sun-dried tomato paste and stir in the wine. Let simmer over low heat, stirring constantly, or until slightly reduced. Stir in the radicchio and season to taste with salt and pepper.

Drain the pasta and transfer to a warmed serving dish. Add the remaining olive oil and toss well with 2 forks. Top with the sun-dried tomato sauce and toss lightly again, then sprinkle with the scallions and toasted pine nuts and serve immediately.

pasta & rice

This gutsy dish is guaranteed to fire up anybody's spirits. Look for a good-quality,

meaty pork sausage, preferably with added herbs.

Macaroni with Sausage, Pepperoncini & Olives

serves 4

1 tbsp olive oil

1 large onion, finely chopped

2 garlic cloves, very finely chopped

1 lb/450 g pork sausage

3 canned pepperoncini, or other hot chilies

14 oz/400 g canned chopped tomatoes

2 tsp dried oregano

½ cup chicken stock or red wine

1 lb/450 g dried macaroni

12–15 black olives, pitted and quartered

scant ¾ cup freshly grated cheese, such as Cheddar or Gruyère

salt and pepper

Heat the oil in a large skillet over medium heat. Add the onion and cook for 5 minutes until soft. Add the garlic and cook, stirring, for a few seconds until just beginning to color. Peel and roughly chop the sausage. Add to the skillet and cook until evenly browned.

Drain and slice the pepperoncini. Stir into the skillet with the tomatoes, oregano, and stock. Season to taste with salt and pepper. Bring to a boil, then reduce the heat and simmer for 10 minutes, stirring occasionally.

Bring a large pan of lightly salted water to the boil. Add the pasta, return to a boil, and cook for 10 minutes, or until tender but still firm to the bite. Drain and transfer to a warmed serving dish.

Add the olives and half the cheese to the sauce, then stir until the cheese has melted.

Pour the sauce over the pasta. Toss well to mix. Sprinkle with the remaining cheese and serve immediately.

This is a useful—and versatile—dish that makes a filling and delicious meal for both

vegetarians and vegans, which can be whipped up in only a matter of minutes.

Rather than a mixture of beans, you could use just red kidney beans or chickpeas.

Penne with Mixed Beans

serves 4

1 tbsp olive oil

1 onion, chopped

1 garlic clove, finely chopped

1 carrot, finely chopped

1 celery stalk, finely chopped

15 oz/425 g canned mixed beans, drained and rinsed

1 cup strained tomatoes

1 tbsp chopped fresh chervil, plus extra leaves to garnish

12 oz/350 g dried penne

salt and pepper

Heat the oil in a large, heavy-bottom skillet over low heat. Add the onion, garlic, carrot, and celery, and cook, stirring occasionally, for 5 minutes, or until the onion has softened.

Add the beans, strained tomatoes, and chopped chervil to the pan and season the mixture to taste with salt and pepper. Cover and simmer gently for 15 minutes.

Meanwhile, bring a large, heavy-bottom pan of lightly salted water to a boil. Add the pasta, return to a boil, and cook for 8–10 minutes, or until tender but still firm to the bite. Drain the pasta and transfer to a warmed serving dish. Add the mixed bean sauce, toss well, and serve immediately, garnished with chervil leaves.

This creamy pasta sauce is a classic Italian recipe, featuring the country's world-famous blue cheese. When buying Gorgonzola, avoid hard or discolored cheese.

Tagliarini with Gorgonzola

serves 4

2 tbsp butter

1½ cups coarsely crumbled Gorgonzola cheese

⅔ cup heavy cream

2 tbsp dry white wine

1 tsp cornstarch

4 fresh sage sprigs, finely chopped

14 oz/400 g dried tagliarini

2 tbsp olive oil

salt and white pepper

Melt the butter in a heavy-bottom pan over low heat. Stir in 1 cup of the Gorgonzola cheese and heat for 2 minutes, or until melted.

Add the cream, wine, and cornstarch and beat with a whisk until well blended.

Stir in the sage and season to taste with salt and white pepper. Bring to a boil over low heat and cook, whisking constantly, until the sauce thickens. Remove from the heat and set aside.

Bring a large pan of lightly salted water to a boil. Add the pasta and half the oil, return to a boil, and cook for 8–10 minutes, or until tender but still firm to the bite. Drain thoroughly and toss in the remaining oil. Transfer to a warmed serving dish and keep warm.

Reheat the sauce over low heat, whisking constantly. Spoon the sauce over the pasta, sprinkle over the remaining Gorgonzola cheese, and serve immediately.

Rich and subtle in flavor and ultra quick to prepare, this dish would make an excellent choice for an informal dinner party.

Pasta with Prosciutto

serves 4

4 oz/115 g prosciutto

4 tbsp unsalted butter

1 small onion, finely chopped

12 oz/350 g dried green and white tagliatelle

⅔ cup heavy cream

½ cup freshly grated Parmesan cheese

salt and pepper

Trim the fat from the prosciutto, then finely chop both the fat and the lean meat, keeping them separate. Melt the butter in a heavy-bottom skillet over low heat. Add the prosciutto fat and onion and cook, stirring occasionally, for 10 minutes.

Meanwhile, bring a large, heavy-bottom pan of lightly salted water to a boil. Add the pasta, return to a boil, and cook for 8–10 minutes, or until tender but still firm to the bite.

Add the lean prosciutto to the skillet and cook, stirring occasionally, for 2 minutes. Stir in the cream, then season to taste with pepper and heat through gently. Drain the pasta and transfer to a warmed serving dish. Add the prosciutto mixture and toss well, then stir in the Parmesan cheese. Serve immediately.

Lemon, ginger, and fresh flat-leaf parsley give

an extra lift to the chicken and pasta in this

Spaghetti with Parsley Chicken

lovely summery dish. Scrub the lemon rind with

a stiff brush to remove any wax before paring.

serves 4

1 tbsp olive oil

thinly pared rind of
1 lemon, cut into julienne
strips

1 tsp finely chopped fresh
gingerroot

1 tsp sugar

1 cup chicken stock

9 oz/250 g dried
spaghetti

4 tbsp butter

8 oz/225 g skinless,
boneless chicken breasts,
diced

1 red onion, finely
chopped

leaves from 2 bunches of
fresh flat-leaf parsley

salt

Heat the oil in a heavy-bottom pan over low heat. Add the lemon rind and cook, stirring frequently, for 5 minutes. Stir in the ginger and sugar, season to taste with salt, and cook, stirring constantly, for an additional 2 minutes. Pour in the stock, bring to a boil, and cook for 5 minutes, or until the liquid has reduced by half.

Bring a large, heavy-bottom pan of lightly salted water to a boil. Add the pasta, return to a boil, and cook for 8–10 minutes, or until tender but still firm to the bite.

Meanwhile, melt half the butter in a skillet over medium–high heat. Add the chicken and onion and cook, stirring frequently, for 5 minutes, or until the onion is soft and the chicken is lightly browned. Stir in the lemon and ginger mixture and cook, stirring, for 1 minute. Stir in the parsley and cook, stirring constantly, for an additional 3 minutes.

Drain the pasta and transfer to a warmed serving dish, add the remaining butter, and toss well. Add the sauce, toss again, and serve.

This super-speedy dish, made mainly from pantry ingredients, tastes fabulous, and

is great for feeding unexpected guests. Serve with a crisp salad and fresh crusty

bread for a filling supper.

Linguine with Bacon & Olives

serves 4

3 tbsp olive oil

2 onions, thinly sliced

2 garlic cloves, finely chopped

6 oz/175 g rindless lean bacon slices, diced

8 oz/225 g mushrooms, sliced

5 canned anchovy fillets, drained and rinsed

6 black olives, pitted and halved

1 lb/450 g dried linguine

¼ cup freshly grated Parmesan cheese

salt and pepper

Heat the oil in a large skillet over low heat. Add the onions, garlic, and bacon, and cook, stirring occasionally, for 5 minutes, or until the onions have softened. Stir in the mushrooms, anchovies, and olives, then season to taste with salt, if necessary, and pepper. Cook for an additional 5 minutes.

Meanwhile, bring a large, heavy-bottom pan of lightly salted water to a boil. Add the pasta, return to a boil, and cook for 8–10 minutes, or until tender but still firm to the bite.

Drain the pasta and transfer to a warmed serving dish. Spoon the sauce on top, toss lightly, and sprinkle with the Parmesan cheese. Serve immediately.

This simple dish takes just moments to make, looks lovely, tastes heavenly, and

contains absolutely no saturated fat—what more could you possibly ask for?

Fettuccine with Smoked Salmon

serves 4

**8 oz/225 g dried
fettuccine**

1 tsp olive oil

**1 garlic clove, finely
chopped**

**2 oz/55 g smoked
salmon, cut into thin
strips**

**1¼ cups watercress
leaves, plus extra
to garnish**

salt and pepper

Bring a large pan of lightly salted water to a boil. Add the pasta, return to a boil, and cook for 8–10 minutes, or until tender but still firm to the bite.

Meanwhile, heat the oil in a large, nonstick skillet over low heat. Add the garlic and cook, stirring constantly, for 30 seconds. Add the salmon and watercress, season to taste with pepper, and cook for an additional 30 seconds, or until the watercress has wilted.

Drain the cooked pasta and return to the pan. Mix the salmon and watercress mixture with the pasta and toss thoroughly using 2 large forks. Divide between 4 large serving plates and garnish with extra watercress leaves. Serve immediately.

Meat & Poultry

The sweetness of the tomatoes contrasts well with the sharpness of the olives in

these tempting skewers, which can be prepared several hours before cooking.

Beef, Tomato & Olive Kabobs

serves 8

1 lb/450 g sirloin steak

16 cherry tomatoes

16 large green olives, pitted

fresh flat-leaf parsley sprigs, to garnish

slices of Italian bread, to serve

BASTE

4 tbsp olive oil

1 tbsp sherry vinegar

1 clove garlic, crushed

salt and pepper

FRESH TOMATO RELISH

1 tbsp olive oil

½ red onion, finely chopped

1 garlic clove, chopped

6 plum tomatoes, seeded, peeled, and chopped

2 pitted green olives, sliced

1 tbsp chopped fresh parsley

1 tbsp lemon juice

salt and pepper

To make the baste, combine all the baste ingredients, with salt and pepper to taste, in a bowl. Cover and set aside until required.

To make the relish, heat the oil in a small pan over medium heat, add the onion and garlic, and cook, stirring frequently, for 3–4 minutes until softened. Add the tomatoes and olives and cook for 2–3 minutes until the tomatoes are softened. Stir in the parsley and lemon juice and season to taste with salt and pepper. Set aside and keep warm or cover and chill in the refrigerator until required.

Trim any fat from the beef and cut the meat into 32 even-size pieces.

Thread 4 pieces of meat onto each of 8 wooden skewers, presoaked in cold water for 30 minutes, or metal skewers, alternating with the tomatoes and olives.

Cook the skewers on an oiled rack over hot coals of a barbecue or under a broiler preheated to high for 5–10 minutes, basting and turning frequently. Garnish with tomato sprigs and serve with the tomato relish and Italian bread.

Broiled pork steaks are given the characteristic Italian treatment, topped with a

tomato and olive sauce flavored with garlic and fresh basil.

Neapolitan Pork Steaks

serves 4

2 tbsp olive oil

1 large onion, sliced

1 garlic clove, chopped

14 oz/400 g canned tomatoes

2 tsp yeast extract

4 pork loin steaks, about 4½ oz/125 g each

³⁄₈ cup black olives, pitted

2 tbsp shredded fresh basil

TO SERVE

freshly grated Parmesan cheese (optional)

freshly cooked green vegetables

Italian bread

Heat the oil in a large skillet over medium heat. Add the onion and garlic and cook, stirring frequently, for 3–4 minutes until softened.

Add the tomatoes and their juice and yeast extract to the pan and simmer for 5 minutes, or until the sauce starts to thicken.

Meanwhile, cook the pork steaks under a broiler preheated to medium–high for 5 minutes on both sides, or until the meat is cooked through. Set the pork aside and keep warm.

Add the olives and basil to the skillet and stir quickly to combine.

Transfer the steaks to warmed serving plates. Top the steaks with the sauce, sprinkle with Parmesan cheese, if you like, and serve immediately with green vegetables and Italian bread.

The fresh taste of sage is the perfect ingredient to counteract the richness of pork.

Pork Chops with Sage

serves 4

2 tbsp all-purpose flour

1 tbsp chopped fresh sage or 1 tsp dried sage

4 lean boneless pork chops, trimmed of excess fat

1 tbsp butter

2 tbsp olive oil

2 red onions, sliced into rings

1 tbsp lemon juice

2 tsp superfine sugar

4 plum tomatoes, quartered

salt and pepper

Mix the flour, sage, and salt and pepper to taste together and spread out on a shallow plate. Lightly coat the pork chops in the seasoned flour, shaking off any excess.

Melt the butter with the oil in a skillet over medium–high heat. Add the chops and cook for 6–7 minutes on each side until cooked through. Drain the chops, reserving the pan drippings, and keep warm.

Toss the onions in the lemon juice, add to the skillet with the sugar and tomatoes, and cook, stirring occasionally, for 5 minutes until tender.

Serve the pork with the tomato and onion mixture and a green salad.

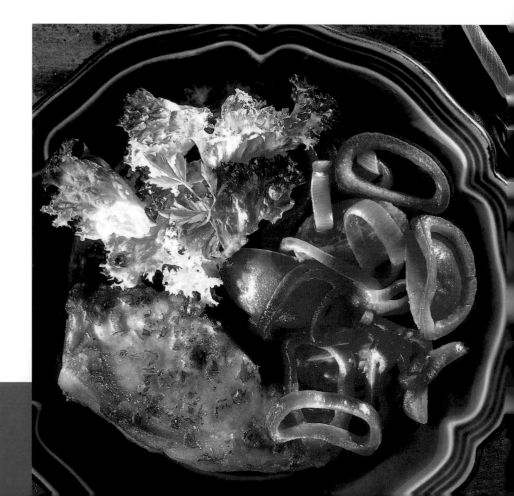

Anchovies are often added to meat dishes in

Italian cooking to enhance flavor. Try 4 minute

steaks, slightly flattened, instead of the scallops.

Scallops & Italian Sausage

serves 4

1 tbsp olive oil

6 canned anchovy fillets, drained and rinsed

1 tbsp capers, drained and rinsed

1 tbsp fresh rosemary, stalks removed

finely grated rind and juice of 1 orange

2¾ oz/75 g Italian sausage, diced

3 tomatoes, peeled and chopped

4 turkey or veal scallops, about 4½ oz/125 g each

salt and pepper

crusty bread or triangles of fried polenta, to serve

Heat the oil in a large skillet over medium heat. Add the anchovies, capers, rosemary, orange rind and juice, sausage, and tomatoes to the pan and cook, stirring occasionally, for 5–6 minutes.

Meanwhile, place the scallops between 2 sheets of waxed paper. Pound the meat with a meat mallet or the end of a rolling pin to flatten to an even thickness.

Add the meat to the mixture in the skillet. Season to taste with salt and pepper, cover, and cook for 3–5 minutes on each side, or slightly longer if the meat is relatively thick.

Transfer to serving plates and serve with crusty bread, or triangles of fried polenta, if you prefer.

Originating in Naples, where it is difficult to find any dish that does not feature the brilliantly colored, rich-tasting tomatoes of the region, this way of serving steak is now popular throughout Italy—and beyond.

Griddled Steak with Tomatoes & Garlic

serves 4

3 tbsp olive oil, plus extra for brushing

1 lb 9 oz/700 g tomatoes, peeled and chopped

1 red bell pepper, seeded and chopped

1 onion, chopped

2 garlic cloves, finely chopped

1 tbsp chopped fresh flat-leaf parsley

1 tsp dried oregano

1 tsp sugar

4 entrecôte or rump steaks, about 6 oz/ 175 g each

salt and pepper

Place the oil, tomatoes, bell pepper, onion, garlic, parsley, oregano, and sugar in a heavy-bottom pan and season to taste with salt and pepper. Bring to a boil, then reduce the heat and simmer for 15 minutes.

Meanwhile, trim any fat around the outsides of the steaks. Season each generously with pepper (but no salt) and brush with oil. Preheat a ridged griddle pan over high heat, place the steaks on it, and cook according to taste: 2–3 minutes each side for rare; 3–4 minutes each side for medium; 4–5 minutes each side for well done.

Transfer the steaks to warmed individual plates and spoon the sauce over. Serve immediately.

These unusual chicken kabobs have the typical Italian flavorings of garlic, tomato, and fresh basil, and the bacon helps keep them moist during cooking.

Skewered Chicken Spirals

serves 4

4 skinless, boneless chicken breasts, about 4½ oz/ 125 g each

1 garlic clove, crushed

2 tbsp tomato paste

4 smoked lean bacon slices

large handful of fresh basil leaves

vegetable oil, for brushing

salt and pepper

salad greens, to serve

Place the chicken breasts between 2 sheets of waxed paper. Pound the meat with a meat mallet or the end of a rolling pin to flatten to an even thickness.

Mix the garlic and tomato paste together and spread the mixture over the chicken. Lay a bacon slice over each piece of chicken, then sprinkle with the basil. Season to taste with salt and pepper.

Roll up each piece of chicken firmly, then cut into thick slices. Thread the slices onto 4 wooden skewers, presoaked in cold water for 30 minutes, or metal skewers, making sure the skewer holds the chicken in a spiral shape.

Brush the skewers lightly with oil and cook over hot coals of a barbecue or under a broiler preheated to high for 10 minutes, or until cooked through, turning once. Serve hot with salad greens.

There is much more to the cuisine of Bologna than the eponymous pasta dish—it is renowned for its rich dishes. The capital of the Emilia-Romagna region, Bologna is nicknamed "la grassa," meaning the fat, rich, and plentiful one.

Chicken with Smoked Ham & Parmesan

serves 4

4 skinless, boneless chicken breasts, about 4½ oz/125 g each

2 tbsp all-purpose flour

2 oz/55 g unsalted butter

8 thin slices smoked ham, trimmed

½ cup freshly grated Parmesan cheese

salt and pepper

fresh basil sprigs, to garnish

Cut each chicken breast through the thickness to open them out, then place the pieces between 2 sheets of waxed paper. Pound the meat with a meat mallet or the end of a rolling pin until they are as thin as possible. Spread the flour out on a shallow plate and season to taste with salt and pepper. Coat the chicken pieces in the seasoned flour, shaking off any excess.

Melt half the butter in a large, heavy-bottom skillet over medium heat. Add the chicken, in batches if necessary, and cook, turning frequently, for 10–15 minutes until golden brown all over and cooked through.

Meanwhile, melt the remaining butter in a small pan. Remove the skillet containing the chicken from the heat. Place a slice of ham on each piece of chicken and sprinkle with the Parmesan cheese. Pour the melted butter over the chicken and return the skillet to the heat for 3–4 minutes until the cheese has melted. Serve immediately, garnished with basil sprigs.

Fish & Shellfish

Although they need cleaning, fresh sardines are a real treat. They are best cooked

very simply—even just plainly broiled or grilled. Here they are flavored with garlic

Italian Sardines

and lemon rind and served with bruschetta. Try broiled bell pepper and fresh basil

as an alternative topping for the bruschetta.

serves 4

1 tbsp olive oil

4 garlic cloves, peeled and lightly crushed but kept whole

1 lb 7 oz/650 g fresh sardines, cleaned and scaled

grated rind of 2 lemons

2 tbsp chopped fresh flat-leaf parsley

salt and pepper

tomato and onion salad, to serve

BRUSCHETTA

4 thick slices ciabatta or other rustic bread

2 garlic cloves, halved

2 large tomatoes, halved

Heat the oil in a large, heavy-bottom skillet over low heat. Add the garlic and cook, stirring frequently, until softened. Meanwhile, for the bruschetta, toast the bread lightly on both sides under a broiler preheated to medium. Transfer to a heatproof plate and keep warm in a low oven until required.

Add the sardines to the pan and cook for 5 minutes, turning once. Sprinkle with the lemon rind and parsley and season to taste with salt and pepper.

To finish the bruschetta, rub 1 side of each slice of toast with the cut side of a garlic clove half, then with the cut side of a tomato half. Divide the bruschetta and sardines between 4 serving plates and serve immediately with a tomato and onion salad.

A griddle or grill pan is perfect for achieving a deliciously crispy outside to the fish while retaining the inner succulence of the flesh without the bother of grilling.

Lemon-Griddled Salmon

serves 4

2 lb/900 g salmon fillet, cut into 4 pieces

juice of 1 lemon

¼ cup butter, diced

salt and pepper

TO GARNISH

fresh parsley or dill sprigs

lemon slices

cucumber slices

Preheat a griddle or grill pan over high heat.

Sprinkle the fish with the lemon juice, dot with the butter, and season to taste with salt and pepper.

Place the salmon on the hot griddle, skin-side down, and cook for 10–15 minutes, turning once when the first side is brown and crusty. The exact cooking time will vary, depending on the thickness of the fillet. When it is ready, the fish should be firm and flake easily when tested with a fork.

Transfer the salmon to a serving dish and serve with herb sprigs and lemon and cucumber slices arranged around the fish to garnish.

The richness of salmon is perfectly balanced by the tangy capers in this creamy herb sauce.

Salmon with Caper Sauce

If you choose the thin, tail-end fillets, they will take the least time to cook.

serves 4

4 salmon fillets, skinned

1 fresh bay leaf

few black peppercorns

1 tsp white wine vinegar

⅔ cup fish stock

3 tbsp heavy cream

1 tbsp capers, drained and rinsed

1 tbsp chopped fresh dill, plus extra sprigs to garnish

1 tbsp snipped fresh chives, plus chive flowers to garnish (optional)

1 tsp cornstarch

2 tbsp skim milk

salt and pepper

lemon wedges, to garnish

new potatoes, to serve

Preheat the oven to 350°F/180°C. Lay the salmon in a shallow baking dish. Add the bay leaf, peppercorns, vinegar, and stock.

Cover with foil and bake in the preheated oven for 15–20 minutes until the flesh is opaque and flakes easily when tested with a fork.

Transfer the salmon to warmed serving plates, cover, and keep warm.

Strain the cooking liquid into a pan. Stir in the cream, capers, chopped dill, snipped chives, and salt and pepper to taste.

Blend the cornstarch with the milk in a small bowl. Add to the pan and bring to a boil, stirring constantly. Boil for 1 minute until thickened.

Spoon the sauce over the salmon and garnish with dill sprigs, chive flowers, and lemon wedges.

Serve immediately, with boiled new potatoes.

Red snapper is a popular fish in Italy, not just because of its wonderful taste but also because it looks so attractive. This is an ideal way of cooking it.

Red Snapper Cooked in a Package

serves 4

4 tbsp extra virgin olive oil, plus extra for brushing

4 red snapper, cleaned, scaled, and heads removed, about 10 oz/280 g each

4 garlic cloves, thinly sliced lengthwise

4 tomatoes, peeled, seeded, and diced

2 tsp finely chopped fresh rosemary

salt and pepper

crusty bread, to serve

Preheat the oven to 400°F/200°C. Cut 4 squares of waxed paper large enough to enclose the fish and brush with a little oil.

Rinse the fish inside and out under cold running water and pat dry with paper towels. Season to taste with salt and pepper. Using a sharp knife, cut 3 diagonal slits in both sides of each fish. Insert the garlic slices into the slits.

Combine the oil, tomatoes, and rosemary in a bowl. Spoon a little of the mixture onto each of the waxed paper squares, then place the fish on top. Divide the remaining tomato mixture between the fish.

Fold up the paper around the fish, twisting it into tiny pleats to seal securely. Place the packages on a cookie sheet and bake in the preheated oven for 15 minutes.

Transfer the packages to warmed plates and cut off the folded edges of the packages. Serve with crusty bread.

This is a perfect example of the healthy Mediterranean diet that nutritionists

recommend—and what is more, it tastes fabulous. Serve with a fresh, crisp salad

for a delicious lunch.

Italian-Style Cod

serves 4

14 oz/400 g canned chopped tomatoes

1 garlic clove, finely chopped

1 tbsp sun-dried tomato paste

1 tbsp sambuca

1 tbsp capers, drained and rinsed

⅓ cup black olives, pitted

4 cod steaks, about 6 oz/175 g each

⅔ cup dry white wine

1 bay leaf

¼ tsp black peppercorns

thinly pared strip of lemon rind

salt and pepper

fresh flat-leaf parsley sprigs, to garnish

Place the tomatoes and their juice, garlic, tomato paste, sambuca, capers, olives, and salt and pepper to taste in a large, heavy-bottom pan over medium heat. Heat gently, stirring occasionally.

Meanwhile, place the cod steaks in a single layer in a large, heavy-bottom skillet and pour the wine over. Add the bay leaf, peppercorns, and lemon rind and bring to a boil. Reduce the heat, cover, and simmer for 10 minutes, or until the fish is tender.

Transfer the cod to a warmed serving dish with a spatula. Strain the cooking liquid into the tomato mixture and bring to a boil. Boil for 1–2 minutes until slightly reduced and thickened. Spoon the sauce over the fish, garnish with parsley sprigs, and serve immediately.

fish & shellfish

This richer version of the traditional dish of mussels cooked with white wine and herbs is ideal for entertaining. Scrub and debeard the mussels earlier in the day and keep in the refrigerator covered with a damp cloth until ready to cook.

Mediterranean Mussels in Cream

serves 4

2 lb 4 oz/1 kg live mussels

2 tbsp butter

1 onion, chopped

2 scallions, chopped

2 garlic cloves, chopped

scant ½ cup dry white wine

3 tbsp chopped fresh flat-leaf parsley, plus extra sprigs to garnish

⅔ cup single cream

Clean the mussels by scrubbing or scraping the shells and pulling out any beards that are attached to them. Discard any with broken shells or any that refuse to close when tapped.

Melt the butter in a large pan over low heat. Add the onion, scallions, and garlic and cook, stirring frequently, for 3 minutes, or until the onion has softened slightly. Increase the heat to medium, then add the mussels, cover, and cook for 4–5 minutes.

Remove the pan from the heat. Using a slotted spoon, lift out the mussels and discard any that remain closed. Set the remaining mussels to one side. Return the pan to the heat, stir in the wine and chopped parsley, and bring to a boil. Cook, stirring frequently, for 10 minutes.

Arrange the mussels in individual serving bowls, then remove the sauce from the heat. Stir in the cream. Pour the sauce over the mussels, garnish with parsley sprigs, and serve immediately.

Vegetables & Salads

This elegant salad would make a good first course. Serve it with Italian bread for mopping up the juices. Bottled artichoke hearts have a better flavor than canned.

Artichoke & Prosciutto Salad

serves 4

9½ oz/275 g bottled artichoke hearts in oil, drained, or canned, drained and rinsed

4 small tomatoes

½ cup sun-dried tomatoes in oil

1½ oz/40 g prosciutto

½ cup pitted black olives, halved

handful of fresh basil leaves

DRESSING

3 tbsp olive oil

1 tbsp white wine vinegar

1 garlic clove, crushed

½ tsp mild mustard

1 tsp clear honey

salt and pepper

Cut the artichoke hearts into quarters and place in a bowl.

Cut each fresh tomato into wedges. Slice the sun-dried tomatoes into thin strips. Cut the prosciutto into thin strips and add to the bowl with the tomato wedges, sun-dried tomato strips, and olive halves.

Reserving a few whole basil leaves for garnishing, tear the remaining leaves into small pieces and add to the bowl containing the other salad ingredients.

To make the dressing, place all the dressing ingredients, with salt and pepper to taste, in a screw-top jar, screw the lid on tightly, and shake vigorously until the ingredients are well blended.

Pour the dressing over the salad and toss together.

Serve the salad garnished with the reserved basil leaves.

This tomato, olive, and mozzarella salad,

presented stack-style and dressed with balsamic

Capri Salad

vinegar and extra virgin olive oil, makes

a flavorful, elegant appetizer.

serves 4

2 beefsteak tomatoes

4½ oz/125 g mozzarella cheese

12 black olives

8 fresh basil leaves, plus extra to garnish

1 tbsp balsamic vinegar

1 tbsp extra virgin olive oil

salt and pepper

Using a sharp knife, cut the tomatoes into thin slices.

Cut the mozzarella cheese into slices.

Pit the black olives and slice them into rings.

Layer the tomatoes, mozzarella slices, olives, and basil leaves in 4 stacks, finishing with a layer of cheese on top.

Place each stack under a broiler preheated to high for 2–3 minutes, or until the cheese has melted.

Drizzle over the balsamic vinegar and oil and season to taste with salt and pepper.

Transfer to individual serving plates, garnish with extra basil leaves, and serve immediately.

vegetables & salads

For this salad, it is worth looking for the authentic cheese, Mozzarella di bufala,

made from water buffalo milk, with its super-creamy texture and superior flavor.

Italian Mozzarella Salad

serves 6

7 oz/200 g young spinach leaves

4½ oz/125 g watercress

4½ oz/125 g mozzarella cheese

8 oz/225 g cherry tomatoes

2 tsp balsamic vinegar

1½ tbsp extra virgin olive oil

salt and pepper

Rinse the spinach and watercress under cold running water and drain thoroughly on paper towels. Remove any coarse stems. Place the spinach and watercress leaves in a large salad bowl.

Cut the mozzarella cheese into bite-size pieces and scatter over the spinach and watercress leaves.

Cut the tomatoes in half and scatter over the salad.

Sprinkle the salad with the balsamic vinegar and oil and season to taste with salt and pepper. Toss to coat the leaves with the dressing. Serve immediately or cover and chill in the refrigerator until required.

The combination of beans and tuna is a favorite with the people of Tuscany. The hint of honey and lemon in the dressing makes this salad refreshing as well as hearty.

Bean & Tuna Salad with Honey Dressing

serves 4

1 small white onion or 2 scallions, finely chopped

1 lb 12 oz/800 g canned lima beans, drained and rinsed

2 tomatoes

6½ oz/185 g canned tuna, drained

2 tbsp chopped fresh flat-leaf parsley

2 tbsp olive oil

1 tbsp lemon juice

2 tsp honey

1 garlic clove, crushed

Place the onion and lima beans in a bowl and mix well.

Using a sharp knife, cut the tomatoes into wedges. Add the tomatoes to the onion and bean mixture.

Flake the tuna with a fork and add to the onion and bean mixture with the parsley.

For the dressing, place the remaining ingredients in a screw-top jar, screw the lid on tightly, and shake vigorously until the ingredients are well blended.

Pour the dressing over the salad and toss together using 2 spoons. Transfer to individual plates and serve.

vegetables & salads

Pesto sauce, which originates from Genoa, is more commonly used as a pasta sauce, but it is equally delicious served over potatoes.

Pesto Potatoes

serves 4

2 lb/900 g small new potatoes

2³⁄₄ oz/75 g fresh basil sprigs, plus extra to garnish

2 tbsp pine nuts

3 garlic cloves, crushed

¹⁄₂ cup olive oil

³⁄₄ cup freshly grated Parmesan cheese and romano cheese, mixed

salt and pepper

Bring a pan of salted water to a boil, add the potatoes, and cook for 15 minutes, or until tender. Drain well, transfer to a warmed serving dish, and keep warm until required.

Meanwhile, place the basil, pine nuts, garlic, and salt and pepper to taste in a blender or food processor. With the motor running, gradually add the oil and process for 30 seconds, or until the mixture is smooth.

Transfer the mixture to a bowl. Stir in the Parmesan and romano cheeses and mix together well.

Spoon the pesto sauce over the potatoes and mix well. Garnish with basil sprigs and serve immediately.

The flavor of broiled or roasted bell peppers

is very different from when they are eaten raw,

so do try them cooked in this way.

Bell Peppers & Rosemary

serves 4

1 tbsp olive oil

finely grated rind of
1 lemon

4 tbsp lemon juice

1 tbsp balsamic vinegar

1 tbsp finely chopped
fresh rosemary or 1 tsp
dried rosemary

2 garlic cloves, crushed

2 red and 2 yellow bell
peppers, halved and
seeded

2 tbsp pine nuts

salt and pepper

fresh rosemary sprigs,
to garnish

Mix the oil, lemon rind and juice, balsamic vinegar, rosemary, and garlic together in a bowl. Season to taste with salt and pepper.

Place the bell peppers, skin-side up, on the foil-lined rack of a broiler pan. Brush the oil mixture over.

Cook the bell peppers under the broiler preheated to high for 3–4 minutes until the skin begins to char, basting frequently with the oil mixture. Remove from the broiler, cover with foil to trap the steam, and let stand for 5 minutes.

Meanwhile, spread the pine nuts out on the broiler rack and cook under the broiler for 2–3 minutes until lightly toasted, turning once. Be careful not to let them burn.

Peel the bell peppers, slice into strips, and place in a warmed serving dish. Sprinkle with the pine nuts and drizzle with any remaining oil mixture. Garnish with rosemary sprigs and serve immediately.

This is an all-Italian take on the traditional Swiss fondue with a feast of three of the country's classic cheeses. It is a great idea for an informal dinner party. You could add olives and cherry tomatoes to the selection of dippers for extra color.

Italian Cheese Fondue

serves 4

1 garlic clove, peeled and halved

2 cups milk

3 tbsp brandy

10½ oz/300 g Gorgonzola cheese, crumbled

7 oz/200 g fontina cheese, chopped

7 oz/200 g mozzarella cheese, chopped

1 tbsp cornstarch

salt and pepper

DIPPERS

Italian bread, cut into bite-size pieces

salami, cut into bite-size pieces

small pieces of apple, wrapped in prosciutto

morsels of roast chicken

Rub the inside of a flameproof fondue pot with the cut side of the garlic halves. Discard the garlic. Pour in the milk and 1 tablespoon of the brandy, then transfer to the stove and bring to a gentle simmer over low heat.

Add a handful of cheese and stir constantly until melted. Continue to add the cheese gradually, stirring constantly after each addition. Repeat until all the cheese has been added and stir until thoroughly melted and bubbling gently.

Mix the cornstarch with the remaining brandy in a small bowl. Stir into the fondue and cook, stirring constantly, for 3–4 minutes until thickened and bubbling. Season to taste with salt and pepper.

Using protective mitts, transfer the fondue pot to a lit tabletop burner. To serve, allow your guests to spear pieces of bread, salami, prosciutto-wrapped apple, and chicken onto fondue forks and dip them into the fondue.

vegetables & salads

Desserts

This classic Italian dish is a luxuriously light and foamy yet rich egg mousse

flavored with Marsala wine. It must be served straight after cooking.

Zabaglione

serves 4

5 egg yolks

½ cup superfine sugar

⅔ cup Marsala wine or sweet sherry

TO SERVE (OPTIONAL)

amaretti cookies

fresh fruit

Place the egg yolks in a large, heatproof bowl.

Add the sugar to the egg yolks and whisk until the mixture is thick and very pale and has doubled in volume.

Place the bowl containing the egg yolk and sugar mixture over a pan of gently simmering water.

Add the Marsala wine to the egg yolk and sugar mixture and continue whisking until the mixture becomes warm—this process may take as long as 10 minutes.

Pour the mixture, which should be frothy and light, into 4 glasses.

Serve the zabaglione immediately with amaretti cookies or fresh fruit, if you like.

This quick version of one of the most widely-loved, traditional Italian desserts

takes just a few minutes to make.

Quick Tiramisù

serves 4

1 cup mascarpone or whole soft cheese

1 egg, separated

2 tbsp plain yogurt

2 tbsp superfine sugar

2 tbsp dark rum

2 tbsp strong black coffee

8 ladyfingers

2 tbsp grated semisweet chocolate

Place the cheese in a large bowl, add the egg yolk and yogurt, and beat until smooth.

Whisk the egg white in a separate dry, grease-free bowl until stiff but not dry, then whisk in the sugar. Carefully fold into the cheese mixture. Divide half the mixture between 4 sundae glasses.

Mix the rum and coffee together in a shallow dish. Dip the ladyfingers into the rum mixture, break them in half, or into smaller pieces if necessary, and divide between the glasses.

Stir any remaining coffee mixture into the remaining cheese mixture and divide between the glasses.

Sprinkle with the grated chocolate. Serve immediately, or cover and chill in the refrigerator until required.

These are cookies Italian style, studded with

nuts and candied peel. Here, white chocolate is

used to coat, rather than the usual semisweet.

White Chocolate Florentines

makes 24

⅞ cup butter

1⅛ cups superfine sugar

1⅛ cups shelled walnuts, chopped

¾ cup whole blanched almonds, chopped

⅓ cup sultanas, chopped

1 oz/25 g candied cherries, chopped

⅛ cup mixed candied peel, finely chopped

2 tbsp light cream

8 oz/225 g white chocolate

Preheat the oven to 350°F/180°C. Line 3–4 cookie sheets with nonstick parchment paper.

Melt the butter in a pan over low heat. Add the sugar and stir constantly until it has dissolved. Bring the mixture to a boil and boil for exactly 1 minute. Remove from the heat.

Add the walnuts, almonds, sultanas, candied cherries, candied peel, and cream to the pan and stir together well.

Drop heaped teaspoonfuls of the mixture onto the prepared cookie sheets, allowing plenty of room for them to spread while cooking. Bake in the preheated oven for 10 minutes, or until golden brown.

Remove the cookies from the oven and neaten the edges with a knife while they are still warm. Let cool slightly, then transfer to a cooling rack to cool completely.

Melt the chocolate in a heatproof bowl set over a pan of barely simmering water. Spread the underside of the cookies with the melted chocolate. Use a fork to make wavy lines in the surface. Let set.

 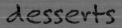

This is an unusual dessert, featuring pasta spirals in a sweet rather than savory role. Teamed with raspberries, the result tastes as good as it looks.

Raspberry Almond Spirals

serves 4

½ cup dried fusilli

4 cups raspberries

2 tbsp superfine sugar

1 tbsp lemon juice

4 tbsp slivered almonds

3 tbsp raspberry liqueur

Bring a large pan of lightly salted water to a boil. Add the pasta, return to a boil, and cook for 8–10 minutes, or until tender but still firm to the bite. Drain the pasta thoroughly, then return to the pan and set aside to cool.

Using a spoon, firmly press 1⅓ cups of the raspberries through a nonmetallic strainer set over a large bowl to form a smooth paste.

Place the raspberry paste and sugar in a small pan over low heat and cook, stirring occasionally, for 5 minutes. Stir in the lemon juice, remove from the heat, and set aside.

Add the remaining raspberries to the pasta and mix together well. Transfer the raspberry and fusilli mixture to a serving dish.

Spread the almonds out on a cookie sheet and cook under a broiler preheated to medium for 2–3 minutes until lightly toasted, turning once. Remove and set aside to cool slightly.

Stir the raspberry liqueur into the reserved raspberry sauce and mix together until very smooth. Pour the raspberry sauce over the raspberry and pasta mixture, sprinkle over the almonds, and serve.

If you prepare these in advance, all you have to do is pop the peaches on the grill

when you are ready to serve them. Use ripe but still firm fruit.

Peaches & Mascarpone

serves 4

4 peaches

¾ cup mascarpone cheese

⅓ cup pecans or walnuts, chopped

1 tsp sunflower oil

4 tbsp maple syrup

Cut the peaches in half and remove the pits. If you are preparing this recipe in advance, press the peach halves together again and wrap in plastic wrap until required.

Mix the mascarpone and pecans together in a small bowl until well combined. Cover and chill in the refrigerator until required.

To serve, brush the peaches with the oil and cook over medium coals of a barbecue for 5–10 minutes, or until hot, turning once.

Transfer to a serving dish and top with the mascarpone mixture.

Drizzle the maple syrup over the peaches and mascarpone filling and serve immediately.

Index